A BOOT UP

THE SURREY HEATHS

Mike Cope

First published in Great Britain in 2010

Copyright text and photographs © 2010 Mike Cope

The author would like to thank *Country Walking* magazine for permission to use extracts from previously published routes.

British Library Cataloguing-in-Publication Data
A CIP record for this title is available from the British Library

ISBN 978 0 85710 006 1

PiXZ Books
Halsgrove House, Ryelands Industrial Estate,
Bagley Road, Wellington, Somerset TA21 9PZ
Tel: 01823 653777
Fax: 01823 216796
email: sales@halsgrove.com

An imprint of Halstar Ltd, part of the Halsgrove group of companies
Information on all Halsgrove titles is available at: www.halsgrove.com

Printed and bound in China by Toppan Leefung Printing Ltd

Contents

How to use this book

The Area

Heathland is an ancient landscape that was largely created by human activity. From the late Stone Age, farmers cleared existing woodland for planting crops, and once the soil nutrients were exhausted, people moved on to cultivate new areas. The grazing of livestock would also have prevented re-establishment of trees and favoured the development of heathland. Over the centuries, heathland has provided fuel, fodder and bedding for local people and their livestock. All of these activities served to maintain the open nature of the heath and prevent its reversion to woodland.

Heathland traditionally occurs on sandy infertile soils, which are acidic and low in plant nutrients. Because the soils are free-draining, they do not hold water for long and heaths are often subject to droughts during the summer months. Only certain plants and trees can survive under these harsh conditions. Heather, gorse, silver birch and Scots pine grow so readily, that if left uncontrolled, they would colonise open heathland.

Surrey supports a significant area of lowland heath - around 3000 hectares (or 13% of the UK total), and about 60% is owned by the military. The Surrey heaths are largely confined to two main areas:

the Wealden Greensand Heaths in the south west and centre of the county and the Thames Basin Heaths in the north west.

The Wealden Greensand Heaths are predominantly dry sites, lying on the Folkestone, Sandgate and Hythe Beds of the Lower Greensand. The notable exception being Thursley National Nature Reserve, and its environs, which support an internationally important mire. The topography of these heaths, in the south west of the county, is more varied than in the Thames Basin - the deeply incised amphitheatre of the Devil's Punch Bowl, Hindhead, being one example. The bulk of the surviving Wealden

Greensand Heaths are centred on or close to Thursley, Hankley and Frensham Commons, with Blackheath an important outlier to the north east.

The topography of the Thames Basin Heaths is generally low-lying land, supporting humid and wet heathland, although, in places, steep hills support dry heath. Three sites, Ash Ranges, Pirbright Ranges and Chobham Common, account for three quarters of the heathland in the Thames Basin. The first two are on MOD land, and access restrictions exist, when red flags are flying.

The Routes

Five of the routes are on the Wealden Greensand Heaths, in the south west of the county, and the remaining five are largely confined to the Thames Basin Heaths in the north west.

All routes are either circular, or a figure of eight design. In the latter case, the option of shortening the route, by completing only one of the loops, is available. They range from 4 ¾ - 9 ¾ miles and are graded from one to three boots – from easy to the more challenging.

Standard grid references are given for accurate location of starting points using an OS map (or mapping web-sites, such as www.multimap.com).

A postcode or 'nearest postcode' is also given to locate the starting point with the aid of an in-car sat nav system. If the starting point is not near a postal address, then the 'near-est postcode' may be some distance away from the actual starting point.

The Maps

Although a thorough description of each walk is given and a sketch map provided, it is advisable to take with you a compass (or sat nav) and a detailed OS map of the area, should you stray from the route or are forced to cut it short. Conveniently, the whole area is covered by the 133, 145 and 160 OS Explorer maps.

Key to Symbols Used

Level of difficulty:

Easy 🌿

Fair 🌿 🌿

More challenging 🌿 🌿 🌿

Map symbols:

🚗 Park & start

⋯⋯⋯ Tarred Road

----- Footpath

■ Building / Town

🍺 Pub

🍽 Refreshments

▲ Landmark

+ Church

▬▬▬ Boardwalk

⋯⋯⋯ Railway Line

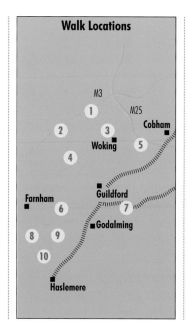

Walk Locations

M3

① ②

M25

③ Cobham ■

Woking ■ ⑤

④

Farnham ■ Guildford ■

⑥ ⑦

■ Godalming

⑧ ⑨

⑩

Haslemere ■

1 Chobham Common

A short 5½ mile ramble across one of the finest examples of lowland heath in the world

Level: 🥾
Length: 5½ miles (9 km)
Terrain: Mainly flat walking along sandy tracks, lowland heath, and through pockets of woodland.
Park and Start: Jubilee Mount car park, Chobham Common
Start ref: SU 972644
Postcode (nearest): GU24 8TP
Refreshments and facilities: The Four Horseshoes, Chobham
Public transport: None to start, but there is a limited train service to Longcross station (Mondays to Fridays only)

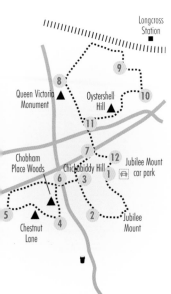

Chobham Common is the largest National Nature Reserve in the South East of England, and one of the finest examples of lowland heath in existence. The tall gorse stands, the heather and the heathland grasses suggest a wild and remote landscape – and so it is. Yet the common is in the heart of suburbia, with the M3 rushing past it, and jets from Heathrow circling above it. The area is recognised across Europe for its variety of birdlife, and over a hundred different species have been recorded here, including the Dartford warbler and the nightjar. It is also one of the best sites in Britain for insects and spiders.

Winter on Chobham Common

1 Locate the information board and take the path on the right, that leads downhill. At the bottom, the path swings to the right, through tall gorse stands and then crosses open heathland. Maintain direction towards a pylon with woodland to the right. When you reach a T-junction, go left towards a lone pine tree and another junction. Go right

The adder is the only venomous snake in Britain and commonly found on heathland or woodland edge habitats. They are distinctly marked with a dark zig zag running down the length of the spine and rarely exceed 60cm in length.

Avenue of oak and birch trees at Jubilee Mount

here along an easily-missed path into woodland. Cross a stile to enter **Jubilee Mount**, then bear left along a wide track, which soon swings right along an avenue of oak and birch trees. When you reach a barrier made from a single metal pole, go straight on along a lane, with houses on the right.

Autumn in Chobham Place Woods

2 At the road, go straight across and follow the public bridleway, along a track that winds uphill with a chestnut trees on the left. Pass under power lines and then fork right towards a junction and a clump of birches.

Chestnut Lane on an autumn evening

(6) Go straight across, and proceed to point 3. Turn left and ascend a small rise (**Chickabiddy Hill**); fork left and then right (after 50 metres) along a track that runs parallel to the M3.

(3) Turn left here, and when you reach the road, go straight across into **Valley End Road**. After 150 metres turn left into **Chobham Place Woods**. Bear half right through the white gate piers and follow the dramatic double avenue of beech and Scots pines to a road.

(4) Turn right along the aptly named '**Chestnut Lane**' and left at the next T-junction.

(5) Bear right at the public bridle way fingerpost, opposite **Sparrow Row**. This track swings to the right and gradually narrows. Turn right immediately before the M3 foot-bridge, then fork left, following the path uphill, and then across open ground, to Windsor Road.

The Dartford warbler is a small bird with a long tail, red eye, and a reddish-brown underside. Its skulking habits make it a difficult warbler to watch, but in summer the male sings from a prominent perch such as a gorse stand or other heathland scrub.

The M3 bisecting Chobham Common

Sandy bridleway across Chobham Common

In 1853, Queen Victoria reviewed 8000 of her troops on Chobham Common, including the famous Light Brigade, prior to their departure to the Crimea. The Victoria Monument, erected in 1901, commemorates this event.

(7) Follow this bridleway as it burrows under the **M3** and then continues to a road. Go straight across and follow the gravel track, ignoring all side turnings, until you reach a T-junction.

Winter on Chobham Common

8 Turn left here for a short diversion to the **monument** dedicated to Queen Victoria. To continue the walk, turn right (at this T-junction) across open heathland, with tracts of ling and bell heather. The track descends and then bends to the right. Go ahead at the next junction, ignoring the right fork, with a railway line in the woods to your left. This line leads to **Longcross station** - the only one in Surrey with a daily service, but no public road access. After crossing a small stream, keep on the main track, ignoring all side turnings.

9 Turn left at the wooden seat, and keep on this track until you reach the double-fenced perimeter road of an **ex-MOD facility**. Turn right here, along **Burma Road**.

Oystershell Hill

10 Take the next right onto the common (by the white MOD sign) along a bridleway. At the next intersection, fork left along an up hill path. Go straight over the next junction, veer left at the wooden seat and descend **Oystershell Hill**.

11 Go left at the next waymarked post, cross a road, and continue under the M3. Fork left, and keep going until you reach a disused car park.

12 Cross the road and then bear immediately right along a wide bridleway, that leads to **Jubilee Mount car park**.

The nightjar is a ground-nesting summer visitor to the heathlands of Surrey. On warm, summer evenings, the male can be heard uttering his mysterious 'churring' call, which resembles the 'buzzing' of power lines. They swoop and flap around their territories with a distinctive flight pattern.

Chobham Place Woods

2 Lightwater and Windlesham

A 7 mile circuit from Lightwater Country Park to Windlesham and back across the fields

The heathland at Lightwater Country Park, is an important fragment of the once vast Bagshot Heath, which stretched to Bracknell and Windsor. Historically heathlands played an important role in rural life, providing trees for timber, gorse and bracken for fuel, and rough grazing for livestock. At 129m above sea level, High Curley Hill is a good place to pick out points of interest. Woking, Ascot race course, Guildford Cathedral and the London skyline are all visible on a clear day.

Level: 🥾 🥾
Length: 7 miles (11.3 km)
Terrain: Undulating heathland, country lanes and urban fringe. A steep climb at the start up to High Curley Hill.
Park and start: Lightwater Country Park main car park
Start ref: SU 917619
Postcode (nearest): GU18 5YD
Refreshments and facilities: The Half Moon, Windlesham
Public transport: Buses 34, 35 from Guildford to Camberley stop at Lightwater

Lightwater Country Park

St John the Baptist church Windlesham

Windlesham Arboretum

Lightwater Country Park

High Curley Hill

Pirbright Ranges

Log staircase up to High Curley Hill

2 Keep ahead past a large glacial boulder, and just before a triangular warning sign (high speed test track), turn left down a wide track that drops steeply downhill. Continue for ½ km and turn left at the next junction. Go through a barrier made from a single pole and at the main road, turn right.

Toposcope on High Curley Hill

1 Leave the main car park near the 'Fitness Trail' and follow the path with purple and orange way-marked posts. The paths dips and rises through woodland. Keep on the main track and when you reach a junction, go straight across up a log staircase to **High Curley Hill**. On a clear day, fantastic views open up of the surrounding towns and countryside.

Heathland on the boundary of MOD land

3 Continue for a few hundred metres along this busy main road and when you see a white MOD board on the left hand verge, cross the road and bear left along an easily missed track. Go under power lines and continue to the wire fence bordering **MOD land**. Turn left and follow the wide track that snakes downhill across open heathland. The track zigzags right and left at the bottom of the hill. Fork left, soon after, through a barrier made from a single pole, past a white house, and along an unmade road. Follow it down to the main road.

Heathland close to the edge of MOD land

4 Turn left and just before the next right turn, cross the road at 'the Folly'. Turn right at the finger-post and continue through a holly-lined track, across a footbridge and along a straight track to a parking area. At the road go straight across, and when you reach the dual carriageway, cross with care into **Blackstroud Lane East**.

5 At the next fork in the road bear left along **Burnt Pollard Lane**. At the T-junction go left along **Hook Mill Lane** and after a few hundred metres turn right along a bridleway.

Bridleway near Hook Mill Lane

St John the Baptist church, Windlesham

6 Follow it for 1km, past a horse-exercising paddock and over the **M3 footbridge**. When you reach the main road, go left into Windlesham.

7 The road goes downhill and around a sharp left hand bend. Take the next public fingerpost right up an alleyway. Cross two drives and continue up the alley to a road.

8 Turn left and then right at the junction and continue past **St John the Baptist church, Windlesham**.

17

9 Turn left after the **Half Moon pub**, and immediately left again at the public bridleway fingerpost. At the next junction, bear right along the public footpath. Cross a stile and keep following the right hand fence which eventually swings left towards another stile. Turn right along a wide track which soon bends round to the left.

Windlesham Arboretum

10 Bear right over the **M3 footbridge**. Keep ahead along a path that soon turns sharp right and follow it to an open area. Go straight across and join the path that merges from the left. Follow this track across **Windlesham Arboretum** with its ornamental lakes and follies. When the track eventually peters out, turn sharp left and then cut right, after 50 metres, across an open area. Turn left

at the fingerpost, and then right, soon afterwards, towards a green gate. Take care as you cross the dual carriageway.

11 Go up the narrow alley and bear right at the road.

12 After 400 metres turn left at the sign for **Lightwater Country Park**. Follow this road (The Avenue), back to the starting point.

3 Woking and Horsell Common

A 6¼ mile circuit that combines a common made famous by H.G. Wells, with a private airport and a Martian sculpture

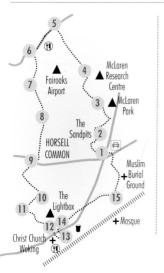

The Martians invaded Earth from the sandpits of Horsell Common, in H.G.Wells' 19th century classic: *The War of the Worlds*. When an adaption of the book was broadcast in 1930s America, it caused a panic-striken stampede out of New York! This walk takes us through pine woods and pasture land, across the open vistas of Fairoaks Airport, and along the towpath of the Basingstoke Canal. The only alien you are likely to encounter on this walk is friendly - a 7 metres high, chrome-plated Martian sculpture in Woking town centre.

Martian sculpture

Level: 🥾 🥾
Length: 6¼ miles (10 km)
Terrain: Mainly flat walking through pine woods, pasture land and urban fringe.
Park and start: The Six Crossroads car park, Horsell Common
Start ref: TQ 013604
Postcode (nearest): GU21 4EF
Refreshments and facilities: The Hangar Café, Fairoaks Airport; The Beacon Café, Christ Church; Wetherspoons, Woking; Sands (at Bleak House) restaurant and bar
Public transport: Bus 472 from Woking station (no service on Sat, Sun or bank holidays)

1. From the car park, walk past the information board and into the pine woods. Go right at the first T-junction and follow the main track as it leads to the edge of a pit, and then swings round to the right. Follow the track along the edge of the pit, and then veer left. **The Sandpits** — where the Martians unleased their Heat Ray — are now straight ahead.

H. G. Wells lived in Woking from 1895 until 1896 and it was here that he wrote The War of the Worlds *and* The Invisible Man. *As two of the greatest pioneering works of science fiction, these early scientific romances remain unsurpassed.*

The Sandpits, Horsell Common

2 Walk past two wooden benches and when you reach a wide bridleway, bear right. Continue over a junction, and then bear left at the green metal barrier in the direction of **Bonsey's Cottages**. Pass several houses and at the bend in the road, go straight ahead into **McLaren Park**.

3 Follow path across parkland, past an ecology lake and then swing right towards the **McLaren Technology Centre**.

4 Cross the footbridge over the Bourne stream, and continue along a wooded path, to **Fairoaks Airport**. Keep walking towards the orange wind sock. The path eventually joins a broad track (**Bonseys Lane**), leading to a main road.

Fairoaks Airport

Fairoaks Airport was built in 1937, when the Air Ministry requisitioned farmland around Chobham for an airfield. During World War II, it was used as a flying school and more than 6000 pilots were trained here.

5 Turn left here and pass the main entrance to Fairoaks Airport and **'The Hangar' Café'**.

6 Continue along the main road, turning left at the yellow **'Fairoaks Airport West Entrance'** sign. The entrance road soon becomes a bridleway which leads along the western perimeter edge of the airport.

Horserider near Fairoaks Airport

7 Pass the edge of the take-off runway, cross two wooden footbridges and walk through a wooded section.

8 When you reach a junction of tracks, keep straight ahead along a broad untarred road, that skirts the edge of Horsell Common. Pass a car park on the left, then turn right into woodland (after 50 metres) along a narrow path.

9 At the road, go straight across into **Cheapside**. After 300 metres, turn left along a public foot-path to '**Collyers Walk and Kettlewell Hill**'. Walk down this alley-way, lined with holly bushes, that runs between the backs of houses. Pass three driveways and when the path starts to descend, take the next right down an alley-way.

10 At the road, go straight across (into **Church Road**) and keep to the right hand footpath. When the road veers left, keep straight ahead.

11 Turn left down the next alley-way, passing a playing field on the right. Turn right at the road and then immediately left (after garages). Continue along this wooded path to a road, where you will find a stunning tree sculpture of Pegasus the winged horse.

The Lightbox is an art gallery and museum, which hosts a huge range of exhibitions, including 'Woking's story', a permanent installation, which explores the fascinating history of the town.

12 Go straight across along the edge of **Brewery Road car park**. Take the footbridge over the Basingstoke canal and pass **The Lightbox** art gallery on the left. Cross the busy dual carriageway, with a cinema and theatre on the right. When you reach **Christ Church** and the town gate, bear left and head for the stainless steel **Martian sculpture**.

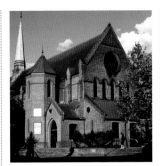

Christ Church, Woking

Christ Church is a lively Anglican church in the centre of Woking with a café, bookshop and conferencing facilities. Alpha courses are run on a regular basis and their home-made scones are some of the best in town.

13 Go left here and just before the dual carriageway, go right down a subway. Note the **tiled mosaic** depicting the 'War of the Worlds'.

Martian Sculpture in Woking town centre

The Sandpits in winter

14 When you emerge on the **Chobham Road**, turn right along the **Basingstoke Canal** towards Sheerwater. Pass under a road bridge, and leave the canal at the next bridge (**Maybury**).

15 Turn left, then immediately right into a carpark on the edge of woodland. Go through a gate, and pass the **Muslim Burial Ground** (on the right). When the track divides, fork right and then go left soon afterwards. Bear right at the T-junction to emerge opposite **All Saints' church, Woodham**. Cross the road and go left towards the roundabout. Take the **Shores Road** exit back to the Six Crossroads car park.

The Shah Jehan Mosque, opened in 1889, is the oldest purpose-built mosque in Britain. It was commissioned by Gottlieb Wilhelm Leitner to provide a place of worship for Muslim students at the Oriental Institute, Woking.

The Muslim Burial Ground

4 Brookwood and Pirbright

*A 9¾ mile walk across Brookwood Cemetery,
along the Basingstoke Canal and down woodland
rides on the edge of MOD land*

In 1851, when cremation was still illegal and London's graveyards were reaching capacity, the London Necropolis company established Brookwood Cemetery on Woking common. It had its own branch railway and special 'coffin trains' brought the dead from Waterloo to Woking. It soon became the largest cemetery in Great Britain and many famous names are buried there, including Dr Gottlieb Leitner, who built the first mosque in England (at Woking). But one grave you won't find there is H.M. Stanley's, the famous

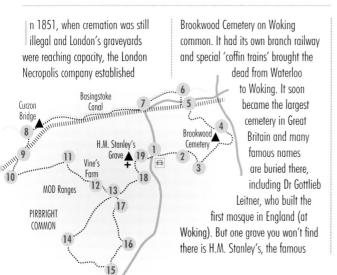

Level: 🥾 🥾 🥾
Length: 9¾ miles (16 Km)
Terrain: Easy walking through cemetery, along canal towpath, and down woodland rides on edge of Pirbright Common (MOD land); one swampy section – boots recommended.
Start ref: SU 947561
Postcode (nearest): GU24 0JT
Refreshments and facilities:
The Cricketers and the White Hart, Pirbright
Public transport: Number 28 Arriva buses from Guildford Friary bus station stop at Pirbright village green

explorer, whose massive roughly-hewn memorial is situated nearby, in the churchyard of St Michael and All Angels, Pirbright.

Pirbright village pond

1 From the car parking area, walk across the green towards the Cricketers pub. Turn left at the road and take the first right up Chapel Lane.

2 At the first bend, bear left at the green signpost and then immediately right. Maintain direction until you reach an embankment and a large ditch. Bear right and follow the ditch until you reach a track.

3 Turn left and follow it into **Brookwood Cemetery**. Turn right at the first major junction (**St George's Avenue**) and follow the semicircular path than brings you out opposite **St Edward's Orthodox church** (where the sacred relics of an English king reside).

The sacred relics of an English king, St Edward the Martyr, who was murdered at Corfe Castle in 978, are enshrined in the Orthodox church at Brookwood.

St Edward's Orthodox church

4 Turn left along **St Cyprian's Avenue** and when you reach a road, go straight across and then immediately left (along **Western Avenue**). At the T-junction, turn right then immediately left into the back entrance of **Brookwood station**.

5 Exit Brookwood station, cross the road and keep ahead towards the **Basingstoke Canal**.

One of the flashes on the Basingstoke Canal

Basingstoke Canal lock

The Basingstoke Canal was built in 1794, to carry timber and agricultural products to London and coal on the return journey. It was never a commercial success and the advent of the railway in the 1830s eventually caused its demise.

6 Gain the towpath and bear left towards **Pirbright Bridge**, where the towpath changes sides.

7 This is the start of the 14 lock flight that raises the canal 95 feet to **Deepcut**. Pass a number of widened out sections of canal (or flashes) and count 11 locks (or 2.5 Km), before you exit the towpath, at **Curzon Bridge**.

*Mountain biking on
Pirbright Common*

8 Go up ramp and then bear left down the approach road. When you reach a road, turn right. At the first bend, branch left up a track and then next left under a **railway bridge**.

9 Follow the track round to the right and then fork left soon afterwards. At the next complex junction, bear left along an uphill path (look out for green sign fixed to a pine tree). When you reach a road go right and cross it at a junction displaying military warning signs .

10 Continue over a 'footbridge' onto **MOD land** and bear left along a downhill track. (N.B. If red flags are flying, follow the road you've just crossed parallel to this track).

11 When you reach a **firing range**, keep ahead through the red and white barrier, and then turn right along an unmetalled lane. Go through a gate and when you eventually reach a junction, maintain direction, taking the track closest to the field.

12 At the next junction, zig-zag left and then right along a tarmac road through a farmyard. Keep on this road until it becomes an unmetalled lane.

In the heart of Pirbright Common

13 When you reach a junction with a sign for '**Vines Farm**', turn right along a wide track. Pass houses on the right, and keep ahead at the next junction. At a complex junction, take the path with the yellow waymark, which eventually merges with a road on the left. Pass **Rails Farm**, and when the road peters out, keep ahead through the wood, following the waymarked post.

14 Take the next left along track on edge of military land. Branch left into wood at yellow waymark (before you reach the red and white barrier). At the next T-junction, zig-zag right and then left along an unmade road (near **firing range**).

Pirbright church tower

15 Take the first bridleway left, passing rhododendrons, ponds and a few houses.

16 Go left up an easily missed footpath; cross a footbridge over **swampy ground** and an open meadow. Re-enter woodland, and continue through avenues of rhododendrons

17 Take the next right along a wide track and at the next junction, go right again along a road.

18 Keep ahead, and take the second footpath left (signposted to **Manor Cottage**). Cross two fields, and when you reach a road, turn right past **St Michael and All Angels' church, Pirbright**.

Hangman's Hill, Pirbright Common

19 Stop to visit the **grave of H.M. Stanley** and the magnificently carved crucifix (war memorial). Follow the lane to a road, cross the village green, and bear left after a play area towards the car park, where the walk began.

H.M. Stanley's grave

5 Wisley and Ockham Common

A 5¼ mile heathland walk encompassing a semaphore tower and a disused airfield

Wisley is the flagship garden of the Royal Horticultural Society (RHS) and undoubtedly one of the great gardens of the world. Its huge plant collection is also diverse, with a comprehensive fruit-growing collection, alpines, vegetables, bulbs as well as herbaceous and woody plants. The Glasshouse is a huge cathedral-like structure with three climate zones, recreating tropical, moist temperate and dry temperate habitats. Opened in 2007 to mark the bicentenary of the RHS, it includes many species of plants, which are internationally classified as rare, vulnerable or endangered.

Level:

Length: 5¼ miles (8.3Km)

Terrain: Relatively flat walking across lowland heath, fields and woodland paths.

Park and start: Wren's Nest car park, Wisley

Start ref: TQ 066589

Postcode (nearest): GU23 6QD

Refreshments and facilities: Boldermere car park café; RHS Wisley, coffee shop

Public transport: A special bus service operates once-a-day between Woking station and Wisley Gardens

1 With the information board in front of you, go through a gate and then turn left along a wide bridleway. After a few hundred metres, fork left and then right at the next T-junction. Continue past a recreational area and pavilion on the left. At the next waymarked junction, fork right to follow a 'permissive horseride'. Continue through oak and birch woodland, as the roar of the **M25** gets progressively louder.

2 After crossing a footbridge, near a large holly bush, the path swings to the right. Keep walking through woodland until you reach a T-junction, with a gate opposite.

Birch trees on Wisley Common

Pond Farm

soon afterwards to pass an information board and dismounting steps for horseriders.

5 Cross the footbridge, over the **A3**, and after 100 metres, bear right at the next wooden fingerpost, marked 'Horse ride'. Proceed up bank and then drop down into a car park, with a café and information centre on the right.

3 Go left here, in the direction of the M25. You will soon see traffic streaming past, the wooden fencing ahead of you. The path swings to the right, and runs parallel to the motorway.

4 Fork right at the next junction along a wide track, away from the M25, and proceed through oak and birch woodland. At the next junction, keep ahead along a wide untarred lane and past a large de-forested area. Pass a house and barn conversion (**Pond Farm**), and continue along a causeway across boggy ground. As you pass another de-forested area, you could imagine yourself in the Scottish Highlands, except for the ever-present roar of the M25. At the T-junction, go left along a metalled road and then fork right

Horse ride near Boldermere car park

Horseriding on Ockham Common

6 Go left at 'The Semaphore Tower' fingerpost and locate a Wisley and Ockham Common information board. Follow the 'Blue Sailor' waymarked posts to the Semaphore tower. Pass through pine woodland, a de-forested area, and then keep ahead at a wide junction. You are now walking through a classic lowland heath area, with sandy bridleways,

horse riders and purple heather. Keep following the 'Blue sailor' waymarks, with a wooden barrier separating you from the 'opposite carriageway'. The track eventually swings to the right and leads you to the **Semaphore Tower**.

The Semaphore Tower, at Chatley Heath, was one of a line of semaphore stations between the Admiralty in London and Portsmouth naval base. Built in 1822, it is now the only remaining tower of the line.

7 Go right at the tower, through a picnic area, and follow the footpath in a south-westerly direction. When you see a lower track on the left, join it at the first opportunity, and maintain direction to a junction. Keep ahead and proceed through woodland until you reach a T-junction, near a clearing. Go left here, and continue to a main road.

Chatley Heath Semaphore Tower

Causeway across boggy ground

(8) Bear left along a road for a few hundred metres, then take the first right, near a house called 'The Gardens'. Cross a stile followed by two more in quick succession. Maintain direction across a field until you reach the runway of **Wisley Airfield** (disused). Cross the runway, between crash barriers, and continue across the field in the direction of a small holding. Notice the large structure on the left, which resembles an alien spaceship.

An emergency landing by a Wellesley bomber on farmland in Wisley during World War II, led to its requisitioning by the MOD for use as an airfield. After the war it became the main flight testing centre for the Vickers-built aircraft.

9 Climb stile and then bear right along right hand edge of field. Keep going past a barn until you reach a farm track.

10 Bear right here and re-cross Wisley Airfield. Go through two gates, past a derelict cottage, and through a wooded area. When you reach a wooden barrier, turn obliquely left, down a public byway.

11 Proceed along wide rutted track through mixed woodland. Maintain direction as the byway becomes a metalled lane.

12 Turn right at the T-junction and re-cross the **A3** via the footbridge. Continue following footpath until you reach the entrance and approach road to Wisley Gardens. Go left here along footpath and maintain direction through woodland until you reach a wooden fingerpost.

13 Go half right here to pass directly in front of the **Wisley Gardens entrance**, shop and café. Keep ahead across picnic area, with main car park on right and smaller overflow car park on left. At the first opportunity, bear left to join the slip

The principle of Occam's razor (lex parsimoniae) states that the simplest explanation is probably the best one, and is attributed to the 14th century logician and friar, William of Ockham.

road out of Wisley Gardens. Keep going until you reach a main road. Go left here and then right after a hundred metres to return to the car park.

Entrance to Wisley Gardens

6 Puttenham Common

*A 4¾ mile ramble across Puttenham Common,
under the shadow of the Hog's Back*

The soil under Puttenham Common belongs to the Folkstone beds of the Lower Greensand series and is rich in iron, which gives it a rusty red appearance. Because the soil is so sandy, it drains freely and is poor in nutrients. North of here the Downs narrow, forming a ridge that rises dramatically above the landscape, called the Hog's Back. Before the Second World War there were many hop fields in the vicinity of Puttenham village, with the picking done by local families or itinerant workers, who travelled about the hop fields of Southern England.

Level:

Length: 4¾ miles (7.7 km)

Terrain: Easy walking across pine and birch heathland (Puttenham Common) and pastoral farmland.

Park and start: Middle car park, Puttenham Common

Start ref: SU 912458

Postcode (nearest): GU3 1BG

Refreshments and facilities: The Good Intent, Puttenham

Public transport: Buses 547 and X65 from Guildford Friary bus station stop in Puttenham

The Good Intent pub

① Locate the information board and exit the car park at the mauve and green waymarked post. The path leads into woodland and then descends into a swampy area. At the junction, keep ahead along a path that threads its way through birch and oak woodland, swings to the right and becomes a broad track. Keep going north, across a boardwalk and past a pond on the right (**General's Pond**).

② Fork right at a junction and follow the mauve and green waymarked posts. The path starts to ascend gradually and the sandy soil underfoot becomes a rusty red. When you reach a complex junction (near the top), keep ahead following the purple waymarked post. Aim for a large pine tree and an open area. Fine views are on offer in all directions, especially northwards to the Hog's Back. The area around the summit was once a pre-**Roman fort** (Hillbury). Keep following the path which descends gradually to a junction.

③ Go left here along the mauve self guided trail. Keep left at the next fork and left again at the T-junction, still following the mauve self-guided trail.

④ When you reach a car parking area, bear right along the **North Downs Way**. The track ascends gradually for some distance with good views of the **Hog's Back** on the left hand side. When you reach the top, keep following the red arrows of the North Downs Way. The pleasant undulating track passes a house before eventually joining a lane. Follow the sunken lane as it descends and joins a road .

Woodland walk across Puttenham Common

Section of the North Downs Way near Puttenham

5 Keep ahead at the next junction along **the Street**, walking through **Puttenham village** past the lines of parked cars until you come to the **Good Intent pub**. The pub has Civil War connections and the signboard depicts a Roundhead soldier, kneeling with his helmet laid beside him and his sword upright in his hands. In the background are the tents of the Puritans' New Model Army. If you wish to investigate the local church, keep ahead past the pub for a few hundred metres).

6 Otherwise turn right opposite the pub along **Suffield Lane**. At the first corner (near the entrance to **Puttenham Priory**) keep ahead over a stile and along a carefully mown elevated walkway to another stile. Take the path along the edge of woodland to a stile. Follow the post and wire fence across open pasture land to another stile. Cut half right across the next field to a stile hidden in a dip. Descend into a hollow with a small pond on the right and follow the right hand edge of the field to a gate and another stile.

Puttenham Millennium signboard with blackbird and hop carvings

Clearing on Puttenham Common

7 Turn right along the road and then leave it at the next bend to go right at the fingerpost; cross over 3 stiles in fairly quick succession. Now the track becomes broader and leads you along a walkway with wide open spaces on both sides. Go through two kissing gates and continue along the gradually ascending track to another kissing gate and into woodland. Keep ahead at the crossroads and then left at a T-junction. Go immediately right uphill and along the edge of a house to a road.

8 Go straight across into **Puttenham Common Top car park** and through the wooden 2 metre barrier. Follow the wide road to the top left hand corner of the car park. Locate the wooden handrail and follow it downhill. When it ends, go right and then immediately left to follow a wider track that leads out of woodland and across open parkland.

9 Ignore all minor turnoffs and when you re-enter woodland again, go left along a broad track following the mauve and green way-marked posts. Keep following this track as it descends downhill and passes close to a road. In a matter of minutes you'll reach the car park with the large holly bush, where the walk began.

Post and wire fence across pastoral landscape

7 Blackheath

A relatively flat 5¾ mile ramble across heathland, field paths and sunken lanes

lackheath common is an area of special scientific interest due to the presence of many rare heathland species such as the sand lizard and ground nesting birds like the woodlark and the nightjar. Lowland heath is a habitat characterized by heather and dwarf gorse. In the stands of Scots pine woodland you can find flocks of goldcrests, long-tailed tits, and other woodland birds. As with many of the Surrey heathlands, Blackheath was used by the Canadian army in World War II as a camp and training ground for the D-Day landings.

Level: 🐾 🐾
Length: 5¾ miles (9.2 Km)
Terrain: Sandy bridleways across lowland heath, field paths and sunken lanes.
Park and start: Blackheath car park
Start ref: TQ 036462
Postcode (nearest): GU4 8RB
Refreshments and facilities:
The Villagers Inn, Blackheath; The Percy Arms, Chilworth
Public transport: Bus 523 from Guildford Friary bus station stops at Blackheath (infrequent service). Buses 21, 22 and 32 stop at Chilworth station.

Verdant signpost

BLACKHEATH

Caravan Park

Dilton Farm

FARLEY GREEN

Lockhurst Hatch Farm

Kiln Hanger

41

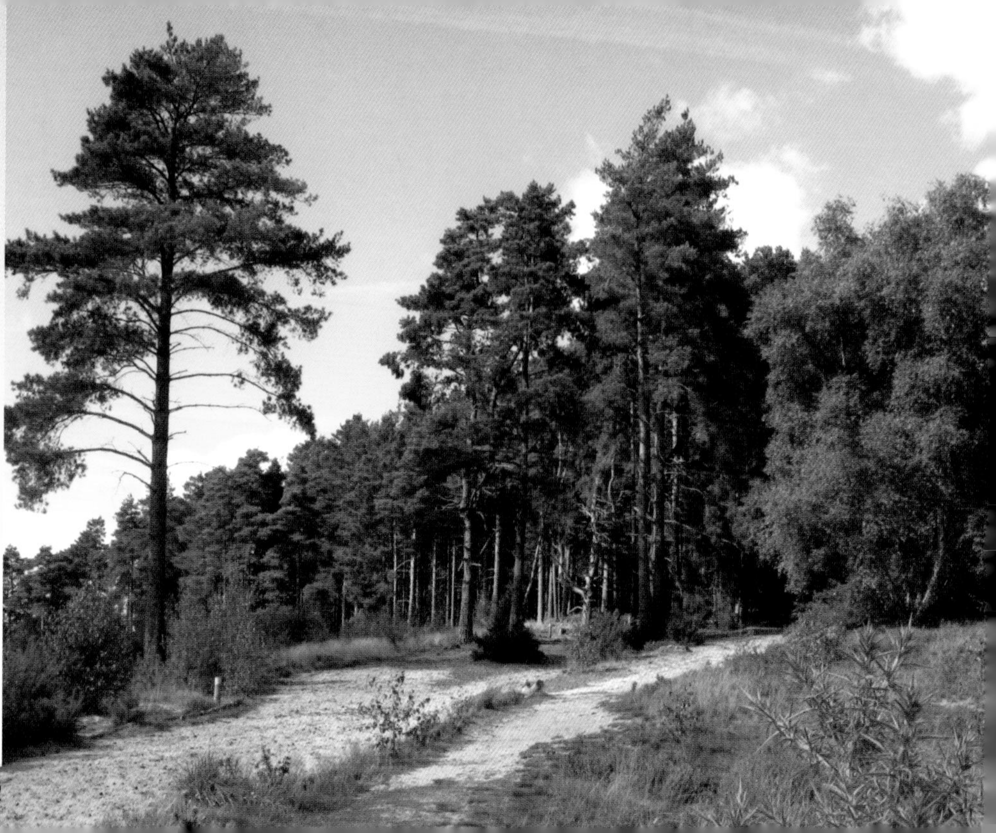

1 With the information board in front of you, bear half right along path next to fire beater post. Keep ahead at the first junction and follow path with Scots pine woodland on the right. Go right at the next junction, then immediately left to join a wide sandy track, waymarked with **light blue posts**. The track narrows

Blackheath Common

and becomes eroded as it enters predominately birch woodland. Keep ahead at the next crossing track. Eventually the track swings to the right and starts to narrow. Maintain direction at the next junction along lane, to pass a dwelling on the right.

2 When the metalled lane veers to the right, keep ahead along a bridleway. After 50 metres, bear right along a narrow sunken bridleway, barely wide enough for a horse to pass. The next 400 metres is heavy going, with small boulders and tree roots to contend with. Eventually the path levels out and gets progressively broader and sandier.

3 Keep ahead at the next junction along a narrow path (ignoring wider track that forks left). The path performs an S-shaped meander, before reaching a junction. Fork left here through an aluminium gate, cross the road and keep ahead along a bridleway towards **Kiln Hanger**.

The Scots pine has been extensively planted in Surrey since the 17th century and is hardy enough to survive on nutrient-poor, sandy soils. The strong, but easily worked, timber has a multitude of uses from telegraph poles to household furniture.

Field path near sunken lane

Looking north towards the North Downs

4 Keep going along a broad bridleway until you pass houses on the left hand side and an ornamental pond. Look left to see wonderful panoramic views of the North Downs. Soon the track starts descending and the banks get steeper.

5 When you reach a junction, go left along a sunken lane (**Ride Lane**). Bear right, after 400 metres, up a flight of steps and over a double stile. Continue across field and cross another stile. The enclosed path leads to another stile and then a lane. Bear left here and then immediately right over a stile and along a narrow enclosed path between fields (a great spot for a break, weather permitting). Climb another stile and drop down to a sunken lane.

6 Bear left and keep going until you reach a metalled lane. Turn right along lane and pass entrance to **Lockhurst Hatch Farm** (on right).

7 Go past a small holding on the left, and keep ahead on a rising path.

8 Fork left at **Dilton Farm** and then immediately left again over a stile, near a large yew. Pause awhile to savour exhilarating views of the North Downs. Continue along a narrow overgrown path which zig zags left and then right, before climbing a steep rise.

9 When you reach a **caravan park**, keep ahead through a kissing gate. Maintain direction at the road and then go immediately left at a wooden fingerpost. Turn right after a few metres and then left to pass house 95. Keep on road through caravan park which swings gradually to the right. Keep ahead at next right hand bend, and locate wooden fingerpost. Turn left through kissing gate

Jubilee signpost

Footpath near Farley Green

and follow path along edge of field. Go through second kissing gate, and cut diagonally across field to third kissing gate and along path between houses to a road.

10 Turn right and keep going until you reach the T-junction at **Farley Green**. Go left along road, and at the first bend, bear right through parking area.

Queen Victoria reviewed her volunteer troops on Blackheath in 1864. To mark this auspicious occasion, the local inn was named 'The Volunteer', but was later renamed 'The Villagers'.

11 Fork immediately right along a broad bridleway. At the next fork, go right in the direction of the blue waymark.

12 Keep on the main track as it swings left (ignoring smaller track on right). Keep ahead at next junction and continue along wide sandy bridleway, until you reach Blackheath car park.

National Trust signpost on Blackheath Common

8 Frensham Common

This 5½ mile figure-of-eight walk circumnavigates a large pond and explores one of the largest expanses of heathland in Surrey

B oth Frensham Ponds are man-made and were created in the Middle Ages to supply the Bishop of Winchester's court with fish during their stays at Farnham Castle. The ponds were drained periodically to trap the carp, which were transferred alive in barrels to local monasteries and kept in 'Stew Ponds' to provide Friday lunch for the monks and local inhabitants. On the walk, you'll encounter the Flashes (a heathery basin, reminiscent of the Scottish Highlands) and the Devil's Jumps (Bronze Age tombs dating from around 500 B.C.).

Sailing on Frensham Great Pond

Level: 🐾 🐾
Length: 5½ miles (9 Km)
Terrain: Flat, sandy heathland, with one ascent up Stoney Jump.
Park and start: Frensham Little Pond car park
Start ref: SU 857418
Postcode (nearest): GU10 3BT
Refreshments and facilities: The Pride of the Valley Hotel, Churt ; The Holly Bush, Frensham; The Barley Mow, Tilford
Public transport: Stagecoach bus no.19 from Haslemere to Aldershot stops at Frensham

1 From the car park, walk eastwards along the road in the direction of **Frensham Little Pond**.

2 Turn right at the public footpath fingerpost, along a track that skirts the pond. Cross a footbridge near a stone arch, and pass to the left of a low stone wall and a stretch of sandy 'beach'. Follow the track through pine and birch trees, with the pond to your right, then fork left.

3 At a National Trust sign, go straight ahead along a track with fences on both sides.

4 When you see a concrete bunker and two Nissen huts, turn sharp right along a wide sandy bridleway.

Frensham Little Pond frozen over

(5) At the road, bear right through **swamp land**. Cross the ford via a footbridge, and turn left into **Graywalls** at the blue waymarked bridleway. At the next junction turn left, with conifers on high ground to the right. Eventually you pass a large private pond on the left. The sandy path bears right uphill into woodland and after several meanders you reach a complex junction of tracks.

Both Frensham ponds were drained during World War II due to suspicions that the Luftwaffe were using them as a navigation aid. Subsequently, they were used for tank training exercises, until they were refilled in 1949.

Steep ascent up Stoney Jump

(6) Take the second left, down a sunken lane with a paddock on the left. The track becomes a metalled road and passes several houses.

(7) Turn left along a resident-friendly horseriding track (P5) to **Tanglewood**. You soon enter an area known as **The Flashes**, a vaste expanse of heather, reminiscent of the Scottish Highlands. Just for a moment you could be forgiven for thinking you'd been transported to Glencoe! The track eventually swings to the left with woodland on the right and open heathland (The Flashes) on the left. Ignore a bridleway on the left, and continue along P5. Pass a meadow on the right and, at a junction of five tracks, take the second right into woodland.

The Devil's Jumps are Bronze age tombs dating from around 500 B.C., described by W.Cobbett in Rural Rides as 'three rather squat sugar loaves'.

8 The path climbs steeply up-hill and, as you gain height, is reinforced with wooden planks. Behind you marvellous views open up of the Flashes and one of its' larger ponds. At the top of the **Devil's Jumps**, you reach a grassy area and a large sandstone outcrop, 'as big as a church tower' (according to W.Cobbett). This is '**Stoney Jump**' - an ideal place to stop and rest. From here you can see layer upon layer of forest, each one getting progressively fainter, until the horizon is lost in mist.

Looking out across 'The Flashes'

9 With your back to The Flashes, bear left at the fire beater post and follow the path down-hill. Bear half left and follow this wide track to the bottom of the hill (with a house on the right).

10 Turn half left again through a metal gate and along a wide track. Bear right at the next junction (near the pond).

David Lloyd George lived for 20 years at Bron y de Farm, Churt, after his stint as Liberal Prime Minister, and also ran a farm shop. The Pride of the Valley hotel, Churt has a restaurant named in his honour.

Frensham Pond sailing club is internationally renowned as a training ground for young sailors who go on to win national and international honours, including one Olympic gold. Sailing for the disabled is another of its specialities, and the unit here is the largest in the UK.

11 Go left at the road, and when you reach a swampy area, you'll realise you've been here before. Go over the ford via the footbridge. At the **Graywalls** junction, go straight on past houses on the left until you reach a turning area.

Sandy track across Frensham Common

12 Turn right here and then take the next left. The track gradually descends to another junction.

13 Go straight ahead and then half-right, following the wire fence along the edge of the pond. At the next junction bear right, still following the wire fence. Walk past a large sandy 'beach', through woodland and follow the path as it bears left away from the water. Continue past cottages and over a junction of tracks to return to the starting point.

View from
Stoney Jump

9 Thursley and Ockley Common

A 5¼ mile board walk and ramble across one of the finest examples of mire and wet heath in southern England

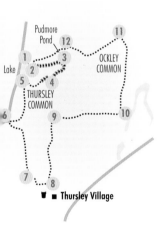

■ **Thursley Village**

Thursley National Nature Reserve is one of the largest remaining fragments of Surrey heath and includes areas of mire, lowland heath, scrub and woodland. The reserve's mixture of mire and wet heath is one of the finest examples of its type in southern England, and is readily accessed by an extensive network of board walks. The boggy pools and ditches provide a rich habitat for dragonfly and damselfly populations and the site also attracts breeding birds associated with lowland heath, including woodlark, nightjar and Dartford warbler.

Level: 🐾 🐾
Length: 5¼ miles (8.5 Km)
Terrain: Board walks across mire and bog areas in Nature Reserve. Sandy bridleways across lowland heath, scrub and pine woodland.
Park and start: Thursley Nature Reserve
Start ref: SU 899416
Postcode: GU8 6LW
Refreshments and facilities: The Three Horseshoes pub, Thursley
Public transport: None to start

Pudmore pond

Board walk across Thursley Mire

① Locate the information board, and take the path to the left of it, with a green waymark, called 'Heath Trail'. Go through pine wood, with lake on right and ignore large bridleway off to left. At first fork, branch left away from lake, and when you reach a green information board, keep ahead on the **Heath Trail boardwalk**.

② This is a wetland bog and you are likely to see white bog cotton. When the boardwalk ends, continue along path, following line of Scots pines.

③ Turn right along boardwalk which leads to a small spinney with information board about dragonflies. Continue along small

path which leads to another boardwalk. You are more than likely to encounter photographers with long lenses patrolling the boardwalk, to capture a close-up of a dragonfly or other invertebrate.

(4) When you reach a T-junction near a fire-beater post, go right. At the next fork, branch right along another boardwalk. Go under two sets of power lines and at next junction, go left along a broad sandy bridleway.

(5) The deep sand, churned up by horses, makes the walk heavy going. Branch right at next fork and when you reach a T-junction, bear right along a wide sandy bridleway.

Sandy bridleway across common

(6) Go left at next T-junction (near road), to pass a dwelling and outbuildings. Keep going along woodland path, ignoring all turnoffs. When track merges from left, branch right soon after, keeping field on right hand side. A hill rises to left of path, and at next waymarked junction, fork left, along wider track. Continue over crossing track and keep following the public bridleway.

Thursley was the childhood home of Sir Edwin Lutyens, deemed the greatest British architect of the 20th century. The classical architecture of New Delhi and the Cenotaph at Whitehall are amongst his achievements.

(7) At next junction, keep ahead along narrow path into woodland. At T-junction, go right towards a house. Turn left at road, in direction of Milford and Godalming. Pass the **village hall** on left and then the **Three Horseshoes pub** on right.

(8) Take the next bridleway left at wooden fingerpost. Go ahead at first junction and then fork left, 5 metres later. The track soon

Fly Agaric mushroom

Thursley village sign

starts to get broader, with a long ridge on the horizon, straight ahead. Maintain direction as a broad bridleway merges from the left and starts to descend slowly. Keep ahead ignoring all turnoffs and when you reach a T-junction with a red sandy bridleway, go right.

(9) Continue on this wide bridleway with power lines running parallel to it. The track starts to ascend slowly, and the sand here is almost as red as Monument Valley - a stark contrast to the bleached sand, encountered earlier on the walk. Continue over crossroads near a fire

Birch woodland on Ockley Common

beater station, at crest of hill. The track starts to drop down and eventually enters pine woodland. Go left at fork, and left again at next crossroads shortly afterwards.

(10) Keep heading northwards, with pine woods on right and open heathland on left. Pass another green information board. At the next major fork, branch left along a bridleway. At the crossroads go left with power lines parallel to track on right.

(11) Pass another green information tion board. The path now starts to narrow and get boggier. Ignore next right and keep ahead on track that swings to right under power lines.

Red sandy bridleway across Thursley Common

12 At T-junction, go left and pass another green information board. To the left, you will see a deep bog and **Pudmore Pond**. Go across boardwalk for 20 metres, and keep going until you reach the next green information board (which you encountered at start of walk). Bear right here and retrace your steps back to the car park.

Line of Scots pine

Pond near car park

10 Hindhead Common

A 5½ mile ramble along the rim and into the heart of a giant Punch Bowl – Surrey's answer to the Grand Canyon

Standing on the rim of the Punch Bowl at Hindhead, just out of earshot of the National Trust tea room, you could be for-

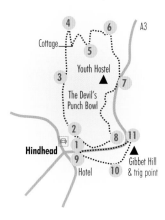

given for thinking that this was Surrey's answer to the Grand Canyon. According to geology, the Devil's Punch Bowl was caused by springs cutting down and back into soft upper sandstone rock to form the largest spring-formed feature in Britain. According to local legend, it was the work of the Devil, who reputedly lived nearby on three small hills at Churt, and often tormented Thor, the God of thunder, by jumping from hill to hill. One day, Thor hurled a handful of earth at the Devil, narrowly missing him and left the huge hollowed-out Punch Bowl, we see today.

Level: 🥾 🥾
Length: 5½ miles (8.7Km)
Terrain: Level path along rim of Punch Bowl and then double descent into heart of Punch Bowl.
Park and start: Devil's Punch Bowl car park
Start ref: SU 891358
Postcode (nearest): GU26 6AB
Refreshments and facilities: Devil's Punch Bowl National Trust café ; Devil's Punch Bowl Hotel, Hindhead
Public transport: Stagecoach bus 238, from Haslemere to Alton college stops in Hindhead (college days only); Countryliner bus 504 also stops in Hindhead

Cyclists at the Devil's Punch Bowl NT café

1 Take the path that leads from the **National Trust café**, past the information board to get your first glimpse of this large natural amphitheatre. When you reach the broad track, bear left and maintain direction until you see a large **telecommunication tower**, where a track merges from the left.

2 Go through a green barrier and an open area, where views open up over the **Punch Bowl**. On its furthermost rim you can see the traffic backing up on the busy **Portsmouth road**. Keep on the main track as it bears to the right, following the rim of the Punch Bowl.

Field in heart of the Punch Bowl

3 At a three way fork, branch right and pass a **memorial stone** before rejoining the main track. The path now starts to descend gradually.

4 When you reach a junction bear sharp right to loop back on yourself, along a gradually

descending path. Go left just before a gate and a field and pass to left of a cottage. Ford the stream and continue up a hollow lane. At the gate, go right up a steadily ascending path.

5 At the junction, go left and continue to ascend. The track bends round to the right. Continue across junction and follow a descending path. Branch right at the next fork.

6 Bear right at crossroads along a rising sandy path. As you gain height, the inside of the Punch Bowl becomes visible again. When you see a green barrier, look right for good views across the Punch Bowl. Maintain direction until you reach a cattle grid and the busy **A3**.

Gorse and pine on eastern rim of the Punch Bowl

The Punch Bowl in winter

7 Continue along path at side of road, which soon veers right away from road and starts descending. When you reach a car park and a metalled lane, cross it and go through kissing gate. Continue down a broad meandering path that leads to the bottom of the Punch Bowl. Go left at a major crossroads, and follow the wide sandy track which descends into the heart of the Punch Bowl. You may see some **wild ponies** here. The wide path ends at an open clearing, where the only way out is up.

8 Locate a lone Scots pine (to your right) and take the path to the left of it, that leads you out of the Punch Bowl. Keep ascending into woodland, until you reach a wooden **flight of steps** and proceed to the Punch Bowl rim. Bear right and continue along the main path and through kissing gate. Bear left at open grassy area to the **National Trust car park** where walk began. Locate entrance to car park and cross busy A3.

Exmoor ponies and Highland cattle are deployed to maintain the heathland by stopping the spread of birch, pine and invasive scrub.

Flight of steps out of the Punch Bowl

(9) Pick up the bridleway that leads over **Hindhead Common**. Go through gate and proceed into open access ground. Continue along main path and across open heathland with gorse stands.

Sir Arthur Conan Doyle lived at 'Undershaw' in Hindhead from 1897 until 1907. It was here that he wrote his most famous novel: The Hound of the Baskervilles.

(10) At the next fork, near bench, go left. Bear left at next junction, cross cattle grid, and maintain direction across complex junction. Go through green barrier to **Gibbet Hill trig point and monument**.

11 Savour the fabulous panoramic views across the Surrey countryside. Retrace your steps to the green barrier and bear right to pick up a newly-laid gravel path and cycle track. Go left and follow gravel path back to the National Trust car park.

In times past, Hindhead was notorious for highwaymen and lawlessness. Gibbet Hill was where murderers and robbers were hung on a gibbet as punishment for their crimes.

Celtic cross on Gibbett Hill